ARTIST TRANSCRIPTIONS®

sonny rollins • art blakey kenny drew

Transcribed by
Masaya Yamaguchi

WITH THE

MODERN JAZZ QUARTET

ISBN 978-1-4768-1456-8

**HAL•LEONARD®
CORPORATION**

7777 W. BLUEMOUND RD. P.O. BOX 13819 MILWAUKEE, WI 53213

Visit Hal Leonard Online at
www.halleonard.com

PREFACE

I would like to commemorate the eightieth birthday of the saxophone colossus, Mr. Sonny Rollins. This transcription collection is based on his early recording, *Sonny Rollins with the Modern Jazz Quartet* (Prestige LP7029/ OJCCD-011-2), made up from the following three sessions:

1. January 17, 1951   Sonny Rollins (tenor sax), Miles Davis (piano), Percy Heath (bass), Roy Haynes (drums)

2. December 17, 1951   Sonny Rollins (tenor sax), Kenny Drew (piano), Percy Heath (bass), Art Blakey (drums)

3. October 7, 1953   Sonny Rollins (tenor sax), Milt Jackson (vibes), John Lewis (piano), Percy Heath (bass), Kenny Clarke (drums)

This recording, *Sonny Rollins with the Modern Jazz Quartet*, is a must-have for all the instrumentalists who are interested in jazz improvisation. We should not overlook that Mr. Rollins learned, absorbed, and crystallized the Charlie Parker reed tradition on these recording sessions. As the saying by a Japanese poet, Basho Matsuo (1644–1694), goes, "Search not for the tracks of the people of old; search for that which they aspired to." Later, Mr. Rollins developed his own conception to the point where he has been called "The Saxophone Colossus." From our current point of view, we all recognize that this early recording is extremely important, educational, and edifying.

Mr. Rollins started out on saxophone under the influences of his idols Coleman Hawkins and Louis Jordan. In his middle teens, he was exposed to the musical revolution, bebop, and Charlie Parker. The legendary jazz trumpeter Miles Davis played the piano in the first session on the tune "I Know." This tune is a contrafact of Charlie Parker's "Confirmation." (Note: On October 5, 1951, they also recorded another contrafact of "Confirmation," entitled "Denial," for Miles Davis's leader session, *Dig* album.)

The importance of this recording for jazz education cannot be overemphasized. Blues and rhythm changes are the important things that we all must learn:

Blues: "Mambo Bounce" (in F), "Scoops" (in B♭)
Rhythm Changes: "Newk's Fadeaway" (AABA in B♭), "No Moe" (AABA in B♭), "The Stopper" (AAB in B♭)

I would like to dedicate this book to all musicians around the world, who love jazz and Sonny Rollins, and wish to enlarge their melodic vocabulary.

Special thanks goes to Rick Hefner and John Zechiel, who helped me to refine my old transcription materials.

山口雅也
Masaya Yamaguchi

CONTENTS

ABOUT THE SESSIONS

Sonny Rollins Quartet
Sonny Rollins (tenor sax), Miles Davis (piano), Percy Heath (bass), Roy Haynes (drums)
NYC, January 17, 1951

"I Know"

Sonny Rollins Quartet
Sonny Rollins (tenor sax), Kenny Drew (piano), Percy Heath (bass), Art Blakey (drums)
NYC, December 17, 1951

"Time on My Hands"
"Mambo Bounce"
"This Love of Mine"
"Shadrach"
"On a Slow Boat to China"
"With a Song in My Heart"
"Scoops"
"Newk's Fadeaway"

Sonny Rollins with the Modern Jazz Quartet
Sonny Rollins (tenor sax), Milt Jackson (vibes), John Lewis (piano), Percy Heath (bass), Kenny Clarke (drums)
NYC, October 7, 1953

"In a Sentimental Mood"
"The Stopper"
"Almost Like Being in Love"
"No Moe"

The Stopper

By Sonny Rollins
Recorded on October 7, 1953

Almost Like Being in Love

Lyrics by Alan Jay Lerner
Music by Frederick Loewe
Recorded on October 7, 1953

Solo
CD Time 0:41

Return
CD Time 2:51

CD Time 3:07

No Moe
By Sonny Rollins
Recorded on October 7, 1953

B-Flat Rhythm Changes

CD Time 1:32

Return
CD Time 2:18

In a Sentimental Mood

By Duke Ellington

Recorded on October 7, 1953

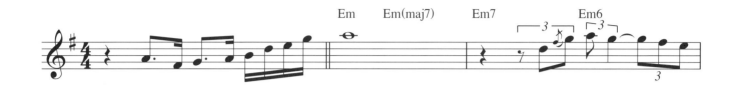

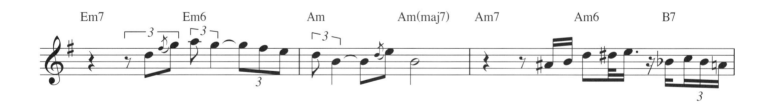

CD Time 1:04

Vibes Solo

CD Time 2:34

This page has been left blank to facilitate page turns.

Scoops

By Sonny Rollins

Recorded on December 17, 1951

With a Song in My Heart

Words by Lorenz Hart
Music by Richard Rodgers
Recorded on December 17, 1951

CD Time 2:15

Newk's Fadeaway

By Sonny Rollins

Recorded on December 17, 1951

1 **B-Flat Rhythm Changes**
CD Time 0:09

Time on My Hands

(You in My Arms)

Words and Music by Harold Adamson, Mack Gordon and Vincent Youmans
Recorded on December 17, 1951

This Love of Mine

Words and Music by Sol Parker, Henry W. Sanicola and Frank Sinatra
Recorded on December 17, 1951

Shadrach

By Robert MacGimsey
Recorded on December 17, 1951

Return
CD Time 1:52

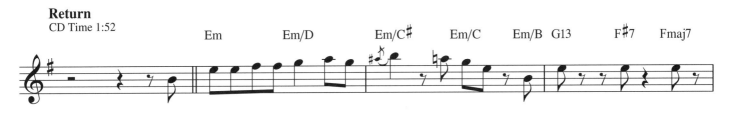

On a Slow Boat to China

By Frank Loesser

Recorded on December 17, 1951

Mambo Bounce

By Sonny Rollins

Recorded on December 17, 1951

I Know

By Miles Davis

Recorded on January 17, 1951

ABOUT THE TRANSCRIBER

Masaya Yamaguchi is not only a musician, but also a conceptualist who established his own system to explore the imaginative formation of musical scales in *The Complete Thesaurus of Musical Scales*, which is a meta-contribution to music pedagogy of a high standard. *Jazz Education Journal* wrote, "It's worth mentioning that this book comprehensively covers all theoretical possibilities in constructing scales. The concept is revealed in many of his writings and compositions (July–August 2002)."

At the end of the twentieth century, Masaya Yamaguchi became the first native Japanese to complete the master's program in Jazz Performance at the City College of New York (M.A. 1999). Because of the reference value of his outstanding achievements, Marquis Who's Who has selected his biographical profile for inclusion in *Who's Who in America*, *Who's Who in the World*, and *Who's Who of Emerging Leaders*. Masaya remains active as an author, guitarist, transcriber, translator, and educator in and around New York City.

Selected Bibliography

Works by Yamaguchi:

Chromaticism in Jazz: Applying Techniques and Concepts. New York: Masaya Music, 2012.

Yamaguchi Improvisation Method. New York: Masaya Music, 2012.

The Complete Thesaurus of Musical Scales. New York: Charles Colin, 2000; Revised by Masaya Music, 2006.

Symmetrical Scales for Jazz Improvisation. New York: Charles Colin, 2001; Revised by Masaya Music, 2006.

Pentatonicism in Jazz: Creative Aspects and Practice. New York: Charles Colin, 2002; Revised by Masaya Music, 2006.

John Coltrane Plays "Coltrane Changes." Milwaukee: Hal Leonard Corporation, 2003.

Charlie Parker "Yardbird" Originals. New York: Charles Colin Publications, 2005; originally printed in 1955.

The Bird Book: The Charlie Parker Real Book. Milwaukee: Hal Leonard Corporation, 2012.

Lexicon of Geometric Patterns for Jazz Improvisation. New York: Masaya Music, 2012.

"Note Groups of Limited Transposition: A Key to Unlocking Multitonic Change Possibilities," *DownBeat*, September 2000.

"A Creative Approach to Multi-tonic Changes: Beyond Coltrane's Harmonic Formula," edited by Jason Sweet and Henry Martin, *Annual Review of Jazz Studies* 12, 2004.

"John Coltrane and Carlos Salzedo: A Surprising Connection," *The American Harp Journal*, Vol. 23, No. 2, Winter 2001, p.59.

Selected Discography

Educational Piano-Roll Series
Monk and Roll: Masaya Yamaguchi. New York: Masaya Music, 2010, EP001

ARTIST TRANSCRIPTIONS®

Artist Transcriptions are authentic, note-for-note transcriptions of today's hottest artists in jazz, pop and rock. These outstanding, accurate arrangements are in an easy-to-read format which includes all essential lines. **Artist Transcriptions** can be used to perform, sequence or for reference.

HAL•LEONARD® CORPORATION

7777 W. BLUEMOUND RD. P.O. BOX 13819 MILWAUKEE, WI 53213

Visit our web site for a complete listing of our titles with songlists at
www.halleonard.com

0113

The Best-Selling Jazz Book of All Time Is Now Legal!

The Real Books are the most popular jazz books of all time. Since the 1970s, musicians have trusted these volumes to get them through every gig, night after night. The problem is that the books were illegally produced and distributed, without any regard to copyright law, or royalties paid to the composers who created these musical masterpieces.

Hal Leonard is very proud to present the first legitimate and legal editions of these books ever produced. You won't even notice the difference, other than all the notorious errors being fixed: the covers and typeface look the same, the song lists are nearly identical, and the price for our edition is even cheaper than the originals!

Every conscientious musician will appreciate that these books are now produced accurately and ethically, benefitting the songwriters that we owe for some of the greatest tunes of all time!

VOLUME 1

00240221	C Edition	$35.00
00240224	B♭ Edition	$35.00
00240225	E♭ Edition	$35.00
00240226	Bass Clef Edition	$35.00
00240292	C Edition 6 x 9	$30.00
00240339	B♭ Edition 6 x 9	$30.00
00451087	C Edition on CD-ROM	$25.00
00240302	A-D CD Backing Tracks	$24.99
00240303	E-J CD Backing Tracks	$24.95
00240304	L-R CD Backing Tracks	$24.95
00240305	S-Z CD Backing Tracks	$24.99
00110604	Book/USB Flash Drive Backing Tracks Pack	$79.99
00110599	USB Flash Drive Only	$50.00

VOLUME 2

00240222	C Edition	$35.50
00240227	B♭ Edition	$35.00
00240228	E♭ Edition	$35.00
00240229	Bass Clef Edition	$35.00
00240293	C Edition 6 x 9	$27.95
00451088	C Edition on CD-ROM	$27.99
00240351	A-D CD Backing Tracks	$24.99
00240352	E-I CD Backing Tracks	$24.99
00240353	J-R CD Backing Tracks	$24.99
00240354	S-Z CD Backing Tracks	$24.99

VOLUME 3

00240233	C Edition	$35.00
00240284	B♭ Edition	$35.00
00240285	E♭ Edition	$35.00
00240286	Bass Clef Edition	$35.00
00240338	C Edition 6 x 9	$30.00
00451089	C Edition on CD-ROM	$29.99

VOLUME 4

00240296	C Edition	$35.00
00103348	B♭ Edition	$35.00
00103349	E♭ Edition	$35.00
00103350	Bass Clef Edition	$35.00

VOLUME 5

00240349	C Edition	$35.00

Also available:

00240264	The Real Blues Book	$34.99
00310910	The Real Bluegrass Book	$29.99
00240137	Miles Davis Real Book	$19.95
00240355	The Real Dixieland Book	$29.99
00240235	The Duke Ellington Real Book	$19.99
00240348	The Real Latin Book	$35.00
00240358	The Charlie Parker Real Book	$19.99
00240331	The Bud Powell Real Book	$19.99
00240313	The Real Rock Book	$35.00
00240323	The Real Rock Book – Vol. 2	$35.00
00240359	The Real Tab Book – Vol. 1	$32.50
00240317	The Real Worship Book	$29.99

THE REAL CHRISTMAS BOOK

00240306	C Edition	$27.50
00240345	B♭ Edition	$27.50
00240346	E♭ Edition	$27.50
00240347	Bass Clef Edition	$27.50
00240431	A-G CD Backing Tracks	$24.99
00240432	H-M CD Backing Tracks	$24.99
00240433	N-Y CD Backing Tracks	$24.99

THE REAL VOCAL BOOK

00240230	Volume 1 High Voice	$35.00
00240307	Volume 1 Low Voice	$35.00
00240231	Volume 2 High Voice	$35.00
00240308	Volume 2 Low Voice	$35.00
00240391	Volume 3 High Voice	$29.99
00240392	Volume 3 Low Voice	$35.00

THE REAL BOOK – STAFF PAPER

00240327		$9.95

HOW TO PLAY FROM A REAL BOOK
For All Musicians
by Robert Rawlins

00312097	$17.50

Complete song lists online at www.halleonard.com

Prices, content, and availability subject to change without notice.

HAL•LEONARD® CORPORATION

7777 W. Bluemound Rd. P.O. Box 13819 Milwaukee, WI 53213

0313

Jazz Instruction & Improvisation

BOOKS FOR ALL INSTRUMENTS FROM HAL LEONARD

AN APPROACH TO JAZZ IMPROVISATION
by Dave Pozzi
Musicians Institute Press
Explore the styles of Charlie Parker, Sonny Rollins, Bud Powell and others with this comprehensive guide to jazz improvisation. Covers: scale choices • chord analysis • phrasing • melodies • harmonic progressions • more.
00695135 Book/CD Pack.........................$17.95

THE ART OF MODULATING
FOR PIANISTS AND JAZZ MUSICIANS
by Carlos Salzedo &
Lucile Lawrence
Schirmer
The Art of Modulating is a treatise originally intended for the harp, but this edition has been edited for use by intermediate keyboardists and other musicians who have an understanding of basic music theory. In its pages you will find: table of intervals; modulation rules; modulation formulas; examples of modulation; extensions and cadences; ten fragments of dances; five characteristic pieces; and more.
50490581 ....$19.99

BUILDING A JAZZ VOCABULARY
By Mike Steinel
A valuable resource for learning the basics of jazz from Mike Steinel of the University of North Texas. It covers: the basics of jazz • how to build effective solos • a comprehensive practice routine • and a jazz vocabulary of the masters.
00849911 ....$19.95

THE CYCLE OF FIFTHS
by Emile and Laura De Cosmo
This essential instruction book provides more than 450 exercises, including hundreds of melodic and rhythmic ideas. The book is designed to help improvisors master the cycle of fifths, one of the primary progressions in music. Guaranteed to refine technique, enhance improvisational fluency, and improve sight-reading!
00311114 ....$16.99

THE DIATONIC CYCLE
by Emile and Laura De Cosmo
Renowned jazz educators Emile and Laura De Cosmo provide more than 300 exercises to help improvisors tackle one of music's most common progressions: the diatonic cycle. This book is guaranteed to refine technique, enhance improvisational fluency, and improve sight-reading!
00311115 ....$16.95

EAR TRAINING
by Keith Wyatt,
Carl Schroeder and Joe Elliott
Musicians Institute Press
Covers: basic pitch matching • singing major and minor scales • identifying intervals • transcribing melodies and rhythm • identifying chords and progressions • seventh chords and the blues • modal interchange, chromaticism, modulation • and more.
00695198 Book/2-CD Pack $24.95

EXERCISES AND ETUDES FOR THE JAZZ INSTRUMENTALIST
by J.J. Johnson
Designed as study material and playable by any instrument, these pieces run the gamut of the jazz experience, featuring common and uncommon time signatures and keys, and styles from ballads to funk. They are progressively graded so that both beginners and professionals will be challenged by the demands of this wonderful music.
00842018 Bass Clef Edition $16.95
00842042 Treble Clef Edition $16.95

JAZZOLOGY
THE ENCYCLOPEDIA OF JAZZ THEORY FOR ALL MUSICIANS
by Robert Rawlins and
Nor Eddine Bahha
This comprehensive resource covers a variety of jazz topics, for beginners and pros of any instrument. The book serves as an encyclopedia for reference, a thorough methodology for the student, and a workbook for the classroom.
00311167 ....$19.99

JAZZ THEORY RESOURCES
by Bert Ligon
Houston Publishing, Inc.
This is a jazz theory text in two volumes. **Volume 1 includes**: review of basic theory • rhythm in jazz performance • triadic generalization • diatonic harmonic progressions and analysis • substitutions and turnarounds • and more. **Volume 2 includes**: modes and modal frameworks • quartal harmony • extended tertian structures and triadic superimposition • pentatonic applications • coloring "outside" the lines and beyond • and more.
00030458 Volume 1 ....$39.95
00030459 Volume 2 ....$29.95

JOY OF IMPROV
by Dave Frank
and John Amaral
This book/CD course on improvisation for all instruments and all styles will help players develop monster musical skills! Book One imparts a solid basis in technique, rhythm, chord theory, ear training and improv concepts. **Book Two** explores more advanced chord voicings, chord arranging techniques and more challenging blues and melodic lines. The CD can be used as a listening and play-along tool.
00220005 Book 1 – Book/CD Pack......................$27.99
00220006 Book 2 – Book/CD Pack......................$26.99

THE PATH TO JAZZ IMPROVISATION
by Emile and Laura De Cosmo
This fascinating jazz instruction book offers an innovative, scholarly approach to the art of improvisation. It includes in-depth analysis and lessons about: cycle of fifths • diatonic cycle • overtone series • pentatonic scale • harmonic and melodic minor scale • polytonal order of keys • blues and bebop scales • modes • and more.
00310904 ....$14.99

THE SOURCE
THE DICTIONARY OF CONTEMPORARY AND TRADITIONAL SCALES
by Steve Barta
This book serves as an informative guide for people who are looking for good, solid information regarding scales, chords, and how they work together. It provides right and left hand fingerings for scales, chords, and complete inversions. Includes over 20 different scales, each written in all 12 keys.
00240885 ....$18.99

21 BEBOP EXERCISES
by Steve Rawlins
This book/CD pack is both a warm-up collection and a manual for bebop phrasing. Its tasty and sophisticated exercises will help you develop your proficiency with jazz interpretation. It concentrates on practice in all twelve keys – moving higher by half-step – to help develop dexterity and range. The companion CD includes all of the exercises in 12 keys.
00315341 Book/CD Pack.....................$17.95

HAL•LEONARD®
CORPORATION
7777 W. BLUEMOUND RD. P.O. BOX 13819 MILWAUKEE, WI 53213

Visit Hal Leonard online at
www.halleonard.com

Prices, contents & availability subject to change without notice.

0113